# RESURRECTION OF A SALESMAN

## LEADERSHIP TIPS FOR PERSONAL GROWTH

# RESURRECTION OF A SALESMAN

## LEADERSHIP TIPS FOR PERSONAL GROWTH

## TRÉ BITTNER

Rev. date: 07/20/2017

To order additional copies of this book, contact:

Xlibris

1-888-795-4274

www.Xlibris.com

Orders@Xlibris.com

559437

PHANTOM RUN PRESS

# Personal Mission Statement

*My mission is **to***

- Treat all people with respect and love including myself.

- Help others in need.

- Achieve financial and career success greater than my own expectation.

- Attain wisdom through development of mind, body, and spirit.

- Know God through deep prayer and goodness of action.

- Honor God by protecting freedom, family, and nature.

- Enjoy life in preparation for my eternal afterlife.

# Dedication

To Mom

and to other American women who work tirelessly to manage career, home, and family with success.

In memory of

- Earle T. Bittner

- Ruth I. Shultz

- W. Murray Hunt

- Neil H. Potter

- Joette L. Litz

# Acknowledgments

I would like to thank that other woman for her spark of inspiration, all my friends and colleagues along the way and those heroes and heroines in military uniform who have courageously defended my freedom and liberty.

# Preface

The sales professional, by example, is a spokesperson for free enterprise and commerce based on his demonstrated commitment to compete for success and recognition of his efforts. Today's sales professional is really no different than his counterpart of yesterday. He is confident, articulate, accountable, honest, intelligent, and more. He champions the cause of his company, and he is proud of his achievements.

Year's back, the famous playwright Arthur Miller wrote a timeless classic about the life, times, and, ultimately, death of a traveling salesman. I chose to title this book as I did not as a mockery of that special story but rather as a salute to the countless number of sales professionals throughout our storied capitalist tradition who have inspired us to reach beyond our own limitations to accomplish great feats. This book does not chronicle my experience as a sales professional or anyone else for that matter. Also, it does not teach or promote sales techniques.

*It simply explores my own personal thoughts on leadership from my perspective as a sales professional.*

Unlike the major character in *Death of a Salesman*, the contributions of sales leaders do not perish. Rather, their valuable lessons about greatness and even the core essence of the human condition rise and flourish, seemingly perpetual, among businesswomen and businessmen and are passed on from one generation to the next.

# Chapter 1

## A Little Bit of This and a Little Bit of That —What leaders are made of

The comparison of the consummate leader as an athlete, diplomat, teacher, and motivator is not surprising. In fact, people of all ages, ethnic and social backgrounds, education, and ability add special ingredients to that recipe that produces genuine leadership talent. Leaders stand out because they are unique and individual. After all, diversity and difference are hallmarks of our own democracy. However, the common bond that all leaders share includes a genuine display of integrity and strong character, which prevails, time in and time out, whenever tested. In addition, true leaders are driven by a deep-rooted sense of intensity to succeed in a noble and earnest manner.

*"Develop your talent to make a positive difference and keep up the intense effort!"*

# Chapter 2

## Leaders Are Helpers

Often, I catch myself pondering about some future great deed or heroic action that I have accomplished as a leader, both in and out of my profession. Interestingly, my thoughts frequently include the people whom I serve with at work and the positive impact that I have achieved with them. No matter what my noble intent is, my "legendary acts" always seem to focus on people.

Ironically, by acting to help others on a regular basis without much thought, you'll condition yourself to think about helping others in a deeper and more strategic way, both in and outside the workplace. Keep in mind that helping people is what we, as business professionals, do for our clients and prospective clients. We help them find solutions.

All of us possess the capacity to help other people. Ultimately, the true leader has achieved his status not through declaration as such but rather through demonstration and action. Even in the midst of an otherwise "off day," always strive to help someone else! Something as simple as holding the door open for someone counts too. Always look for opportunities to help people and do not resist the need for occasional change! If, at times, you experience burnout with your favorite charitable or volunteer activity, discover a new way to give of yourself. Helping others helps you achieve self-fulfillment and satisfaction.

*"Continue to help and lead! Your great acts will pay worthy dividends, and others will truly appreciate your contributions."*

# Chapter 3

## Leaders Do Persevere

Amid constant challenge and frequent stress, you can rise to achieve greatness. Remember, beautiful rainbows follow harsh storms, but they're well worth the wait. Seemingly, we are consumed by worry and anxiety that are not always the result of actual events but rather the result of our own attitudes and negative thoughts. Learning to manage our own attitudes in the midst of challenge can help us increase efficiency and instigate successful results. Like rainbows, success usually follows failure to some extent. If we do not allow ourselves the opportunity to learn by trial and error, we will not enjoy or appreciate the benefits of our hard work. Sales professionals complete activities like prospecting for new clients on a regular basis with much rejection. However, the thrill of discovering and selling a qualified prospect is worth all the "no's" in the world.

In addition, I urge all of you to look beyond the challenge at hand to find effective solutions. Ultimately, looking for solutions beyond the challenge at hand involves visualizing a productive and positive outcome. Thus, the desired end result does help to justify the means.

*"Look up, step forward, and do good!"*

# Chapter 4

## It's All about Perspective

What I like best about sales management is the opportunity to share my perspective with my colleagues and hopefully achieve positive impact in the process. I am truly amazed at the incredible effort that my peers demonstrate on a daily basis throughout their years of devoted service to our company. However, between personal and professional responsibilities, we can easily neglect to appreciate the natural beauty that surrounds us and fills our world, or even ignore our own feelings as they pertain to other people, places, and events. In other words, we lose sight of our sensitive side or that part of us that can help us strengthen our character, boost our morale, and grow as human beings.

Those leaders among us who have experienced deep joy, consistent success, and true happiness understand the impact of perspective on their own lives. They embrace and accommodate any opportunity to express themselves in loving and caring ways through generous acts of kindness, and they take time to "smell the flowers." (I do recommend that you roll up your pants' legs if you plan to kneel while admiring the flowers when dressed in business attire, especially if you decide to do so in between sales calls.) Leaders work hard to develop wisdom that helps guide their lives.

*"Strive to exercise perspective in order to brighten your journey!"*

# Chapter 5

## Leaders Are Truly Humble by Nature, and They Like to Recognize and Reward Their Supporting Cast

Memorable people demonstrate a special ability to make everyone feel important and worthy of recognition and accolade. Ironically, it is not fame that drives talented leaders to achieve stardom; it is the deep-rooted desire to impact others in a very profound way and to leave a lasting impression on humankind no matter what their professional endeavor is.

Salespeople exemplify humility by virtue of their professional experience whereby they ask for the opportunity to earn their client's business. However, rejection is a real and necessary part of developing effective leadership skills because it fortifies our resolve and teaches us to be thankful for our blessings in the process. To the sales professional, rejection is the catalyst for humility; and humility, in turn, helps productive leaders continue to grow, prosper, and serve others.

Exhilaration is much more than the excitement of achieving a successful result; it is the feeling that we experience when we do good deeds for others, especially when we reward and recognize those people who routinely support our cause. Discipline yourself to recognize others on a frequent basis! Remember, people love to be surprised with pleasantries no matter how small. Also, you will win many new and lasting friends by earning their support and admiration through generous and honest acts.

*"Never, ever forget to thank and recognize people who support your efforts! To rally around their cause is to boost yours."*

# Chapter 6

## Leaders Make Mistakes and Sometimes Act Selfish. After All, They Are Only Human

Given our fierce drive to compete, we sometimes compromise ourselves and others through inappropriate or unfair behavior. "To err is human," but failure to acknowledge our mistakes and "right our wrongs" will diminish our ability to establish trust and influence positive results. Too often, I observe business professionals who are stubborn and refuse to admit their error. They equate success with dominance and absolute power. Sadly, that type of behavior is counterproductive and inhibiting. True leaders admit their mistakes, correct them, and then continue to strive to achieve productive relationships.

The opportunity to express our own free will in a capitalist society is both a gift from God and a demonstration of good faith by our fellowman. We must respect and nurture our right to conduct business at our personal discretion by behaving in an ethical and honest manner. When we err and we know that we erred, we must act swiftly with courage and fortitude in order to right our wrong and ultimately to preserve free trade and enterprise.

*"Learning to manage our egos to our own advantage requires self-awareness and introspection. Know thyself!"*

# Chapter 7

## Leaders Are Attractive People

Sure, all of us look like a million dollars in formal business attire, but our real beauty lies beneath the suit deep within our spirit and personality. Leaders are attractive because they nurture a special aura that radiates with positive energy and draws others to them. You know that you are in the presence of a charismatic leader because his handshake is firm but reassuring and his smile is friendly and inviting.

The chivalrous leader is stoic, mannerly, and even noble. This demonstration of chivalry is probably his most noticeable link to his leader brethren from past generations. Leaders have proven through time that hard work, talent, and appropriate conduct are essential qualities for personal and professional success.

*"Show us your attractive side each and every day!"*

# Chapter 8

## Leaders Are Loyal Supporters

The heart of team spirit is nurtured by a strong sense of loyalty and commitment to a cause. Promoting the cause of your company, charity, or a loved one is that principle that inspires leaders to overcome adversity, defy the odds, and produce stellar results. However, do not feel guilty if you change teams from time to time along the way. Loyalty is conditional upon circumstance. Sometimes, the reality of change itself redirects our sense of loyalty.

Lasting and unyielding loyalty to God, people, and country is paramount; but if you decide to switch companies (even to the ones that compete) for the right reasons, you can continue to earn respect by demonstrating trustworthiness and true honor. No matter what team you find yourself representing, always strive to exemplify integrity and the "golden rule" on a consistent basis.

*"As my decorated and retired Marine Corps officer brother says, 'Semper fidelis,' leaders are 'always faithful' to their cause."*

# Chapter 9

## Leaders Care and They Share

I think that the opportunity and ability to attain wealth and affluence are blessings. They are meant to be shared with others. The power to do good and serve the fellowman is the leader's highest honor and most revered privilege. His single greatest tribute to his own legacy is the lasting impression he made on others for his personal and philanthropic contributions. Making money is not about obtaining material pleasures, exclusively. Rather, it should propagate responsible and considerate actions to improve the lives of others and to fortify our democratic values.

However, all of us can lead by sharing more than money. No money is required to volunteer your time to a worthwhile cause, drive a neighbor to the grocery store, or "lend an ear" to a friend in need of an empathetic listener. And do not forget to count your blessings by remembering to sympathize and care for the sick child who might not live to experience the joy of life or the senior citizen who worked hard all his life only to retire to financial distress.

*"Look for an opportunity to help others in need!"*

# Chapter 10

## No Title Required

Ironically, many of us assume that leadership is reserved for those people who hold management or supervisory titles, exclusively. Actually, leadership is not "bestowed upon" or "awarded to" anyone simply because they manage other people. Rather, leadership is a state of reference that special people earn based on their performance and behavior as it affects people. Leaders do not "draw a line in the sand" to separate themselves from others, but their followers do draw that line out of respect and admiration for their positive impact and contributions.

All of us—regardless of our position, title, or level of authority within our company—can enrich others through effective leadership skills. The contributions you share with your organization's cause and the impact that you achieve with other people define the extent of your "leadership quotient."

However, the ultimate magnitude of leadership influence is multidimensional in that one great speech or one genuine act of unselfish kindness does not measure greatness. Hard work on a consistent basis; a proven commitment to be the best; mentoring others in order to support their development; and continually helping colleagues, family, and friends are attributes that define the memorable leader, the leader that others emulate, follow and imitate.

*"Come one, come all, answer the call for leadership!"*

# Chapter 11

## It Is Not the Price of Leadership but Rather the Privilege of Leadership

Formerly, I viewed the responsibilities and sacrifices inherent to leadership as a price you pay in order to guide and influence others. Now, I realize that the opportunity to help other people improve themselves and achieve success is not measured by any price. To me, the connotation that price defines leadership is selfish. True leaders earn their renowned reputation through selfless acts of sharing. Leaders share their talent, wisdom, and dedicated work ethic to support the cause of their colleagues and their company.

They are humbled by the trust and loyalty that others bestow upon them, for true honor is the leader's staff. Ultimately, the satisfaction you feel by helping other people attain their goals far exceeds any "price" that you might pay in order to facilitate that success as a leader. Therefore, leadership is a real privilege.

*"It is not the recognition for which we choose to lead. It is the potential for profound and lasting impact of our actions on our beneficiaries that inspire our desire to lead."*

# Chapter 12

## Leaders Learn from Other Leaders

I am a strong proponent of the Socratic method of learning or learning through personal interaction between student and teacher. Nowhere is this more appropriate than in business because experience attained by trial and error becomes the knowledge that leaders covet, then share, and pass on to the next generation of aspiring leaders.

Look at those people whom you respect, admire, and trust to facilitate and guide your personal and professional development. Ironically, you should welcome mentors from diverse educational, social, and vocational backgrounds too, for these people might very well reveal profound solutions, ideas, and perspective like you never imagined.

While simple, I have learned some great lessons about leadership throughout my journey in sales:

— to have a friend, you must first be a friend.

— the system (company or government) can never be fair; only the people in the system can be fair.

— you are as good as the best, but you are no better than the rest.

— work by the golden rule or treat others as you want to be treated.

— ultimately, business is all about managing relationships effectively.

(This is the single greatest lesson that I have learned during my professional life to date. I like to refer to it as the "supreme axiom" of commerce.)

*"Approach life as an opportunity to learn and to lead, for greatness is a measure of both action and reflection!"*

# Chapter 13

## Leaders Love Liberty

All of us who are fortunate enough to be born in this great nation of the United States of America enjoy free will by divine plan and through America's unyielding commitment to preserve it as a right for every citizen.

Leaders flourish in a free society because they were raised to respect the sanctity of sacrifice that others eagerly volunteered in order to protect and maintain our freedom and safety.

We may have taken the pleasures/luxuries of modern society like transportation and other technologic innovations for granted in our youth, but as adults, we value the progressive contributions from leaders like our grandparents and our parents who worked relentlessly to propel America forward. Their resolve to preserve our freedom and build an even greater nation became their legacy to us.

However, none of our rights including freedom of speech and movement would be possible without the heroes and heroines in uniform including our military, police, and firefighters who have answered the call of duty without reservation, on demand, and too often with the loss of their own lives.

Leaders love liberty because they are free to aspire and achieve greatness.

*The Pledge of Allegiance resonates far beyond the classroom. Remember it, respect it and embrace it!*

# Chapter 14

## Leaders Appreciate "The Other Side of Serious"

No matter what the situation is, sometimes you need to laugh and laugh hard. Granted, laughing at someone's funeral is probably not appropriate, but I must admit that I have been attacked by the "giggles" by surprise on more than one occasion. (And yes, I was "attacked" at a funeral once.)

Daydream about fictitious events where you are the star of hilarious comedic situations! You can generate your own laughter without insulting or hurting someone else because it is downright cruel to laugh at others under the wrong circumstance.

Ultimately, gloomy days can become happy ones when you choose to laugh and have some fun.

Try my easy three-step plan to overcome anxiety and beat the blues!

1. Smile first thing in the morning in front of the bathroom mirror for thirty seconds minimum.

2. Laugh hard at lunch even if you must force yourself. (Remember, you can create your own humor in your mind.)

3. Stare at yourself in the mirror for another thirty seconds at the end of the day, then wink.

*"Allow your lighter side to shine through and don't hesitate to act quirky! You can help others with your lighthearted and goofy charm."*

# Chapter 15

## Leaders Are Prolific Daydreamers

While I often tease myself that I am a "legend in my own mind," there is some merit to that thought. (Heck, I have achieved superstardom as a hero, lover, athlete, business tycoon, statesman, and healer throughout the years, even if only in my mind.) Seriously, daydreams can prove to be truly self-inspiring, especially when those fantasies instigate positive action that benefits other people. Sure, if you don't work to make your dreams a reality, then you will not enjoy the true rewards that result from earnest effort and calculated risks.

As I mentioned previously, the more you condition yourself to actually help others, the easier it becomes to think about new ways to help others. Reverse that line of thought for daydreams. The more you expand your fantasies in your mind, the more likely you are to initiate them or at least attempt to initiate them.

Sometimes, it might be said that our daydreams are simply ghosts that link us to an unfulfilled past. While that might prove true to an extent, those same dreams can help motivate us to aspire and achieve new goals. No matter what our station in life is, it is never beyond our grasp to create new dreams and to follow them.

*"Where there is life, there is hope. Never abandon your aspirations and always run to the rainbow, for that is where the colors meet to greet your dreams!"*

# Chapter 16

## Leaders Find Strength in Character

The human condition thrives on the self or the ego. Through instinct, our existence is manifested in self-gratification. However, through intellect, socialization, and spirit, we realize that our lives are guided by greater purpose.

Character is the defining quality that separates extraordinary leaders from ordinary people. It is natural to respond to disappointment, rejection or exhilaration, and success with both negative and positive emotions and actions; but ultimately, the power of character neutralizes our ego to help us facilitate responsible and respectable behavior.

Leaders earn respect and a strong following for the character they demonstrate on a consistent basis during times of challenge and change.

*"The legacy of a leader is molded by his character."*

# Chapter 17

## Leaders Marvel at the Power of Value

As I learned earlier on in my managed care career from a senior sales executive, value is determined by measuring the relationship between quality and cost. Increasing quality while maintaining or reducing cost increases value.

Unfortunately, many consumers in today's economy define value by cost, exclusively. However, the effective leader, no matter what his or her profession is, realizes the impact of quality on his success and growth. While it might appear obvious that those people who achieve stellar results do so by working diligently to develop and expand their own talents, their commitment and dedication to produce superior quality through their vocation is no easy task.

Successful people extend their demonstration of quality beyond their work or professional careers deep in to their core persona. They elevate quality to new levels through their relationships with other people. These people even stand out in a crowd because they act polite and confident, and they are amiable and well-groomed even if they choose to wear simple or plain attire.

*"The valuable leader treats every penny and each person like gold."*

# Chapter 18

## Leaders Walk a Straight Line

No, they are not boring or careless or reckless for that matter. However, leaders do understand the importance of order in their lives. They approach their craft, relationships, and other pursuits in an organized manner. Sometimes cautious, sometimes daring, they are reasonable and detail oriented on a consistent basis. Ironically, their sense of order is often expressed in their own unique and individual way.

Although they might not define it in my terms, all leaders embrace "Bittner's linear equation of success":

*The more organized you are, the more efficient you become, the more productive you will be, and, thus, the more profit you will see.*

(organization + efficiency + productivity = profitability and success )

While leaders reflect on their past, they always move forward in the right direction with conviction and determination.

*"Tow the line, but draw the map according to your own vision."*

# Chapter 19

## Leaders Are Intuitive

While many people might define a leader by his or her ability to positively impact others via his outgoing personality or presence, the foundations of penetrating leadership are introspection and intuition. The expression "Know thyself" is critical to the development of an aspiring leader because if you are not comfortable with who you are as an individual, you will not be able to effectively understand and impact others for the better.

Deep prayer or meditation and personal reflection will foster growth of your spirit, and your spirit, in turn, will illuminate through your sense of intuition. Not that you should make uninformed decisions based on your intuition alone; however, you should use your intuition to guide your decisions, especially when you are attempting to resolve difficult situations involving people directly, or you are in search of answers to complex challenges of significant consequence.

For those leaders who are exceptionally creative or imaginative by nature, be careful not to confuse your imagination with your intuition! Sometimes, it can be tempting to make judgments about people, places, or things based on bias or an overactive imagination void of fact.

*"Listening to our inner selves will help us manage our external environment."*

# Chapter 20

## Consistency Is the Constant

Although their lives do change as they progress, leaders enjoy success because their approach to personal and professional endeavors is consistent. Consistency helps a leader gain momentum by building a foundation for growth. Actually, the values that a leader learns at any early age, including the love that he receives and shares with family and friends, comprise the core of consistent thought and behavior. Know a leader; and you will know that his commitment, effort, and talent are consistent at work and at leisure.

*"Count on someone whose words and deeds are consistently good!"*

# Chapter 21

## Leaders Demonstrate an Extrafirm Resolve

While great sales professionals are often characterized as persistent and determined to succeed by overcoming obstacles and achieving their goals, the same can be said for all leaders no matter what their vocation.

Regardless of the hurdles or disappointments along the way, leaders are consistently resolute, and they never quit. Granted, they lose some "skirmishes," but they win more battles than not because they think positive and they act with intense passion. Also, people who achieve their dreams and attain stellar results are truly resilient.

Not to say that leaders do not commiserate or allow self-pity to enter their thoughts from time to time, because they are not always upbeat and confident. However, they do not allow tough times to destroy their resolve. Rather, they use them to fortify it.

Consult mentors and read books by inspirational leaders to mold and nurture your resolve and to expand your commitment to be the best person possible!

*"Fear of failure is never a leader's real threat, for absolute resolve permeates the deepest part of his spirit."*

# Chapter 22

## Leaders Live Their Roles

Leaders are more than true students of their chosen vocation or craft. As I learned from President Ronald Reagan, successful people actually live the roles they assume in life. Whether an actor, statesman, business professional, or teacher, people who lead with impact prepare for success through hard work; then they act upon that preparation.

Leaders balance action with reflection; but they do so with passion, energy, intellect, spirit, and conviction. Ultimately, they lead by example including courage, tenacity, and a shining display of good manners. Like my mom always told me, "Soap is cheap, but manners are free." My dad taught my brother and me the value of a firm handshake at the ripe age of five. In addition, my brother and I were not permitted to move from the dinner table without first asking to please be excused. We can preserve our American tradition of strong character and willpower by teaching our children the true value of good manners.

*"Choose your role, study the script, then act the part like no other before you!"*

# Chapter 23

## The Essence of Leadership

The dictionary defines it as one or more people who follow another person. I define leadership as the ability to influence and impact others in a profound and positive way. Basically, leaders are decent people with much integrity, courage, and respect; but in a grander display, they act as heroes and heroines to many. They are unselfish, and they are always eager to help others. Leaders stand aside with humility to observe other people receive accolades and praise even when they were the real impetus of another's success.

Many words can be used to describe a leader, but for me, "goodness" is the strongest adjective of them all. Goodness is guided by eternal purpose and principle. It might seem apparent that only select or chosen people demonstrate an innate talent for effective leadership ability. However, all of us enjoy the capacity to lead via the human bond, which manifests goodness through divine will. Ask a leader; and he will tell you that while he acknowledges his own talent, work ethic, and the impact of loved ones, ultimately, he credits a higher power for the blessing of success. Leaders look upward to Mr. Destiny for wisdom and strength. (I use the affectionate nickname of "Mr. Destiny" for God because I do believe he is the perfect architect of our lives.)

Remember, how we choose to lead is not as important as the positive outcome that we strive to accomplish!

*"Lead by example with passion and conviction on behalf of all!"*

# Conclusion

Leaders are people that do command genuine respect, and now, more than ever, they are in urgent demand. We live in a world that seems more complicated and confusing each day, especially as we are exposed to those world events that cause us true heartache and concern. However, it is refreshing and inspiring to feel the comfort and security of those great deeds and contributions from even greater people.

I encourage all of you to both remember and reflect on the past in order to continue tradition and learn valuable lessons. More important, concentrate and focus on the future with hope and promise for an even better world. After all, the very best leaders are keen visionaries who demonstrate an exceptional ability to guide time itself by looking forward through the collective eyes of other people. Leaders intuitively anticipate what others need; then they conceive, develop, and implement innovative solutions for perplexing challenges. They simply walk in many different shoes and sizes all at once, hence, their ultimate allure.

Although short on words, I hope my book has proven "long" on impact with you, my reader. I trust you will pursue your aspirations with unyielding passion, develop and exercise your special talents, and always look for ways to help others in need; for leadership talent is innate in each one of us.

Although the sun does not shine bright every day, be prepared to seize its energy when it radiates with brilliance, and remember, whenever you see a rainbow, be sure to run toward it because that is where the colors meet to greet your dreams!

Godspeed.